VOLLEYBALL

PHYSICAL EDUCATION ACTIVITIES SERIES

Consulting Editor:
AILEENE LOCKHART
University of Southern California
Los Angeles, California

Evaluation Materials Editor:
JANE A. MOTT
Smith College
Northampton, Massachusetts

3/77

PHYSICAL EDUCATION
ACTIVITIES SERIES

VOLLEYBALL

GLEN H. EGSTROM
University of California, Los Angeles

FRANCES SCHAAFSMA
*California State College
at Long Beach*

SECOND EDITION

WM. C. BROWN COMPANY PUBLISHERS
Dubuque, Iowa

Copyright © 1966, 1972 by
Wm. C. Brown Company Publishers

Library of Congress Catalog Card Number: 70-180511

ISBN 0-697-07052-2

Printed in the United States of America

Contents

Preface

The change in the game of volleyball from an informal small group activity with minimal skill requirements to a dynamic, highly competitive sport requiring an extensive repertoire of special skills has occurred in relatively recent times. Its acceptance as an Olympic sport has dramatically focussed attention upon the necessity for rigorous conditioning and the acquisition of a variety of complex skills.

Although there is still a wide range in the emphasis upon skill and strategy in various parts of the country there has been a widespread improvement in the level of play. It is the purpose of this book to present volleyball as a sport requiring the high levels of speed, strength, endurance and coordination necessary to any demanding team effort. The skills presented in the following pages are considered as fundamental to effective play and should not be considered too advanced for the average player.

The strategy and play patterns are representative of the many variations which can be taken advantage of by special player talents. The book, in its intent, is a guide to better play and will, we hope, stimulate novice players to acquire skills which will continue to improve the generally accepted level of play in our educational and recreational institutions.

Special thanks are extended to those individuals who have demonstrated the skills which are presented in the text, Miss Sharon Peterson, Miss Barbara Brushert, Mr. Dodge Parker and Mr. Richard Lindgren.

What Volleyball Is Like 1

Volleyball has long been recognized as one of the most popular participant sports in the United States. Estimates of participation, however, include play which is variously modified to meet social and environmental restrictions, i.e., number of players on a side, court size, net height, etc. The game, played in strict accordance to the official rules, is still limited to a relatively small, but growing, number of enthusiasts. Because the game can be and is played by so many, with great differences in amount of skill, there is general lack of appreciation for correct ball handling during the early learning stages. This weakness is gradually being overcome with clinics, training films and additional publicity which stresses "power" volleyball.

The official rules call for six players on a team and the object of the game is to cause the ball to strike the floor on the opponent's court or to cause an opponent to engage in faulty play. A net, suspended across a 60' x 30' court, provides the playing area. Each team is arranged with three players across the front court near the net and three players behind them across the back court.

The game starts with the players facing the net and the right rear player of the team which won the toss stepping out of bounds behind the court into the 10' wide serving area. The server strikes the ball sharply causing it to fly over the net to the defensive team. The receiving team must then field the serve and return it over the net using no more than three hits. This pattern of three hits is basic to the game. Ideally, the first hit is a pass to the center forward player, called the setter. The setter then passes the ball into the air and parallel to the net so that one of the front flanking players can drive the ball into the opponent's court, preferably with such force that it cannot be returned before it hits the floor. If the receiving team is successful in returning the ball to the serving team, then the servers have three hits in which to put the ball back over the net. This exchanging is called a rally and continues until a team commits a fault or fails to return the ball over the net.

When a team wins the service all of its players rotate one position clockwise in order to bring a new server to the right rear corner. A team must hold its rotation order until the ball is served at which time rapid rearrangements enable players to move into advantageous positions.

During this rearranging there can be some confusion since a back court player may move to the front court as a setter. This is legal, but the back court player may not spike the ball unless he moves into the back court and must be in proper rotation position prior to each service. This ruling prevents one or two players from dominating the game. In coeducational play at least one of the three hits must be made by a girl for the same reason.

Points are scored only by the serving team and one point is awarded for each rally which is successful for the servers. If the receivers win the rally they then become the servers and are eligible to score points. A game is completed when a team scores 15 points or playing time has elapsed. A tie at 14-14, however, calls for additional play until one team succeeds in gaining a two point advantage. A match consists of a two out of three game series.

The sport of volleyball is well suited to today's living since it can be played and enjoyed by people of all ages. It also provides the opportunity to acquire a group of skills which can be used for many years in an almost injury free environment. At the same time it provides a highly competitive, action filled exercise pattern for large muscle groups. The level of competition and activity is regulated by the skill level of the players but it can be appropriately strenuous at all levels.

Most of us recognize that we feel better if we have regular, vigorous activity in which we can find relief from the tensions of work. Exercise contributes to the maintenance of muscle tone, helps control weight and provides much needed exercise for the heart muscle. For many years community Y.M.C.A. programs have sponsored "noontimers" volleyball for businessmen. Here an individual has opportunity to relax in friendly, good-natured play with peers who are also seeking an outlet for their need for activity. During recent years the development of more adequate community recreation facilities has led to increasing numbers of evening volleyball periods for adults. These programs are usually co-recreational and so provide the married couple a chance to engage in a sport together. School programs have also recognized the growth of facilities and interest and are making an effort to prepare their students with sufficient skills to enable them to feel a sense of accomplishment while engaging in play.

At the beach the mobility of the game is well demonstrated. Two uprights, a net, a ball and 180′ of rope (or lines scratched in the sand) provide a court which can be set up in 10 minutes. Many beaches, in fact, have courts or at least uprights in place throughout the year in order to meet the growing demands for recreational volleyball.

The following chapters will provide you with insight into the nature and requirements of this sport which brings pleasure and healthful exercise to so many people in the country.

Skills Essential

for Everyone

2

The game of volleyball, when properly played, requires that the participants make specific adaptations to the artificial environment and value system of the game. This requirement is often overlooked by beginners who rarely identify the problems whose solutions lead to increased efficiency and effectiveness in play.

The dimensions of the courts (30' x 60') and the barrier (7'4¼" for women and 8' for men) indicate that short, quick movements and jumping are critical skills which are required in order to adapt to the physical limitations of the court. The light, well inflated ball necessitates the development of ball handling skills which result in a high degree of control both in direction and magnitude.

Moving quickly on the court depends upon adequate strength and endurance coupled with alertness. The strength and endurance requirements are quite specific and should be met through drills or game situations that involve the body in the exact movement roles appropriate to the game and with ever increasing work demands. If there are adequate levels of strength and endurance, the readiness of the individual becomes the critical element. Too often players stand erect, hands at their sides, waiting for the ball. When it comes they must raise their hands and arms, bend at the knees and then start to move. Logically the time taken to prepare to move is wasted, since the preparation could have been incorporated into the waiting stance. The "ready" position for volleyball is one in which the knees are slightly bent, hands are carried about waist height, the body

Figure 1—Ready Position

3

If the hand contacts the ball on a serve in the manner shown in the diagram, in which direction will the ball be delivered?

is balanced and attention is focused on the ball. Caution: when moving to field a ball, take your steps *before* you begin to bend and reach—this will result in better control of the movement and you will be able to handle "low" balls much easier.

Jumping in volleyball is usually performed near the net. This means that the jumping style must be adapted to keep the player from touching the net. The tendency to jump forward results in fouls. It is important, therefore, to learn that you must move to the place where you wish to jump and then transfer essentially all of your momentum so that it goes up parallel to the net. Beginning players who jump and fly through the air become a hazard to teammates and a help to opponents.

Ball handling skills are probably the most critical skills to be developed since the circumstances for their application change very rapidly during play. The following skills are presented with the knowledge that extensions and modifications will be dictated by the demands of each play situation.

The Serve

The serve is extremely important because only by retaining the service can a team score points. It is necessary to do more than just get the ball over the net. Each player on the team should be able to place a serve accurately anywhere in the opponent's court. Any time you can put the opponents on the defensive with your serve, you are that much closer to winning the game.

The first consideration when serving is to be aware of body position. The server must remain in the 10' service area and may not step on a boundary line of that area. Avoiding service faults is of prime importance, and the best remedy for hitting a ball into the net, ceiling or out-of-bounds is purposeful practice. Thinking through the entire serve, taking a deep breath, exhaling half of it and relaxing before executing the movement take just a few seconds and should result in a good serve accurately placed.

The Overhand Serve—This serve is used by the majority of leading players because it can be placed accurately and if delivered correctly will

Figure 2—The Overhand Serve

"float" or wobble, putting the opponent on the defensive because he will have to make a quick adjustment to receive the ball. It often causes the receiver to make either an off-center or illegal pass.

The right-handed server stands facing the net with the left foot slightly forward. The ball is tossed with both hands, to prevent it from spinning, to a height 2' to 3' above the head and about 1½' forward of the shoulder. The right arm is brought back and the wrist and elbow cocked. As the elbow leads the way, it is extended so that the player is reaching with a fairly straight arm as the ball is contacted solidly with the heel of the hand. If the ball is tossed too far forward the hand contacts it above the center line of the ball and it prabably will not clear the net. On the other hand if the ball is tossed too close to the head it will be punched to the ceiling or perhaps hit out of bounds. It is important to hit behind and slightly below the center of the mass of the ball to avoid sending it out of bounds to either sideline. To make the ball float and drop it is necessary to keep it from spinning during delivery. To accomplish this the ball is hit with no wrist action after contact. Contacting the ball in line with the upper arrow in figure 3 will cause a down-

Figure 3—Result of Contact upon Ball Flight

ward flight—a net serve. Contacting the ball in line with the lower arrow will usually result in a serve which skims the net and is difficult to field.

The Underhand Serve—This is a good consistent method for getting the ball over the net; however, it does not have the effect of the overhand serve because it is generally not difficult for the defense to receive and pass. It is easy to learn to place the underhand serve but seldom does it put your opponents on the defensive.

Stand facing the net, knees bent, with the left foot forward and the left arm extended across the front of the body. The ball rests on the palm of the left hand. The right arm is swung straight back, then forward to strike the ball with the heel of the hand or the flat fist (palm forward). The head should be bent slightly forward as this helps to keep the ball lower so it will skim the net. As the ball is struck you step forward with your right foot as you follow through with the swing of your right arm. Again it is important to contact the ball solidly and directly at the point which will result in a proper trajectory.

Figure 4—The Underhand Serve

The Forearm Pass

Recent changes in the interpretation of the rules regarding the pass have created the necessity for widespread use of the forearm pass as the technique for passing serves and spikes. The rules state only that the ball must be clearly hit. This, however, requires a judgment by the referee and in most competitions two hand, open handed plays are ruled as violations on receiving the serve or ball coming over the net. The ball handling technique which is herein described as the "set" has also seen widespread use as the overhead pass (see figure 6) with only minor modification. Since the trend is away from this technique we are listing the forearm pass as the technique of choice for passing and fielding.

Hopefully, a clear interpretation statement on the problem will be included in the rules.

The forearm pass requires that the ball strike both forearms simultaneously and be directed high into the air toward the setter who will in turn position the ball for the spiker. This pass, shown in figure 5, is aptly named since the ball rebounds from the flat surface which is placed in its path. Swinging the arms to meet the ball will result in an unnecessarily high pass which can hit the ceiling or travel out of bounds.

To get into position for the forearm pass the player must move quickly to a position in line with the flight of the ball. Too often the novice reaches for the ball and then attempts to move to it. A better technique is to move the body first and then do whatever minor arm positioning is necessary to achieve an accurate well controlled pass. *Run and reach, don't reach and run.*

Figure 5—The Forearm Pass

Once the body is in position the forearms are brought together with the thumbs parallel and the fingers of one hand in the palm of the other hand. This placement will result in a relatively flat surface for rebound should the ball be misjudged. The angle of the forearm will in a large measure dictate the angle of the return flight of the ball. If the forearms

Have a partner throw the ball into the net. Using the forearm bounce pass, can you play the ball over the net? Can you do this on 3 out of 5 trials? on 5 consecutive trials?

are perpendicular to the path of the incoming ball it should rebound exactly away in the path from which it came. Thus the angles of incidence and reflection become critical to controlling the ball. Bending the elbows sharply will often cause the ball to fly back over the head. This is usually undesirable except when it is necessary to play the ball back over the head to save it.

Considerable practice is necessary before a player learns appropriate positioning of the forearms for reaching to the sides, over the head and for very low balls. The frustrations in learning the skills are, however, usually forgotten in the satisfactions which come as a result of accompilsh-ment of the technique.

A less frequently used variation is the one arm pass or "dig" which is used as a desperation measure when the ball is nearly out of reach. This pass is difficult to control and should not be used as a preferred technique. It requires much more practice and is considered an advanced skill.

The Net Recovery—If the ball is hit into the net on the first or second contact it is possible to keep it in play if it can be bounced into the air again. The forearm pass or the dig is used for this recovery shot. When it is performed correctly it looks easy and smooth. The most important consideration in this shot is watching where the ball strikes the net. A ball landing near the top of the net will drop almost straight down. If it hits the center of the net it will rebound out a foot or two before dropping. A ball that contacts near the bottom of the net will most often be held by the net momentarily before rolling out and down.

The player watches the ball and with experience and practice can determine where to position himself for its recovery. He turns his side to the net and crouches in order to contact the ball as close to the floor as possible. If it is to be the second hit the player should try to bounce the ball up and back to avoid hitting it back into the net. This also gives his teammate a better opportunity to spike or place the ball on the third hit. If it is to be the third contact with the ball, the player attempts to hit it up and over the net. This particular shot is difficult to achieve but can be done with practice.

The Set Up

This skill is used to take a pass and alter its flight so that the ball will be put into the air at a location where the spiker can drive it down onto the opponent's court. It is possibly the most critical portion of the pass-set-spike pattern since it depends upon precise execution for an ac-curate set up to the spiker. The cardinal rule for the setter is *to get into*

Figure 6—The Set Up Pass

position under the ball. The head is up, looking at the ball, the elbows are out, the hands are up, the knees are bent and one foot is slightly advanced. See figure 6.

The fingers are cupped slightly so that the fingers and thumbs contact the ball at the same time. The ball *never* touches the palms of the hands during the set. The wrists are laid back with the palms facing upward. Index fingers and thumbs should form a triangular window that the setter can look through to see the incoming ball. The tips of the thumbs are about 6″ apart. Setting involves the whole body and as the ball is contacted the ankles, knees, hips, shoulders, elbows and wrists each provide a portion of the effort that is expended on the ball. Recall that a "clean" set cannot be made easily if the elbows are kept close to the body.

The ball is most easily set in the direction the body is facing and therefore body position is of prime importance. If the setter is under the ball some alternative moves are possible. By taking a slight step back just before the ball is contacted he can set up the spiker he faces. If he takes a step forward he can easily set up the player behind him. The setter should delay taking this step until the last second in order to keep the opponent blockers unaware of who will be receiving the ball. The setter places the ball between 1½′ and 2′ from the net and at least 5′ above the net. As in the pass, the ball should arch, hang and then drop directly in the position desired. Through the use of signals the setter can let his spikers know to whom he is giving the ball and where they will receive it. By setting up the ball at either corner of the net it is easier to spread out the blockers on the opponent's team. At advanced levels of play the setter may set "short sets" or "shoot sets" as well as regular sets to pre-planned net positions. These are deceptive to the opponent, but take much practice and coordination between setter and spiker.

Even though the setter does not receive a perfect pass from the back line and it is necessary for him to move under the ball he should be able to set up his spikers for the kill. The second ball always goes to the front set unless he calls for help from another player.

The setter should know his spikers' capabilities and know where they like the ball placed. With purposeful practice, teamwork will evolve that permits the players to use numerous variations of the set and thus improve their effectivness.

The Spike

The spike constitutes one of the most difficult to coordinate acts found in any sport. The player must be able to run, jump high, time a moving ball, hit it solidly, and at the same time try to place it in a certain spot. It is a spectacular skill to observe and even more spectacular to perform.

The spike is varied by almost every player to his individual preference; however, a great deal of study has been made of this skill and there are certain actions which must be performed to accomplish a hard, fast drive on the ball.

The two-foot take-off is the accepted starting procedure. The spiker adjusts his position at the start in order to run in a straight line toward the net and ball rather than approaching from an angle. The run is made from 10' to 12' back and varies among players from a long stride to short steps or a glide. The crouching position is assumed in order to give more impetus to the jump. The jump is made approximately 2'-3' behind the ball so it is above the head and about a foot in front of the spiking shoulder. The player does not come up under the ball. As he jumps both arms are flung up and the upper trunk twisted sideways to the net so the spiking right arm is back. The left arm is carried higher for balance. As the left arm is driven down, the shoulders become parallel to the net. The elbow leads as the spiking arm whips forward and it acts as a pivot to prevent the arm from hitting the net. The arm straightens as the wrist snaps forward to drive the heel of the hand into the ball. With enough height to the jump, the ball can be hit with the heel of the open hand as the hand and fingers are snapped forward. The ball is directed over the net and down into the court.

The player must be prepared for his spiked ball to be blocked, in which case it would drive right back down at him. He must also be balanced to prevent falling into the net or over the center line. The defense for these problems is handled in the follow-through. The player lands with knees bent and elbows close to the body for balance and with hands ready for a quick dig on a blocked ball. See figure 7.

Even if the ball is set up too far back from the net for the conventional spike, it still can be attacked in much the same manner. The ball is contacted slightly behind the head with the heel of the hand. The fingers are held rigid and the heel of the hand strikes sharply upward, across the rear of the ball, thus imparting top spin. The top spin causes the ball to drop in a sharper arc.

Common faults in spiking are hitting the ball out of bounds or into the net. These faults can be remedied with the development of proper timing, a sufficiently high jump, and proper position of the hand as contact is made with the ball. Timing is critical since hitting the ball during

Figure 7—The Spike

its ascent will tend to result in hitting under the center of mass of the ball. This will result in a trajectory which will carry the ball out of bounds. Hitting the ball too late during its descent can result in a net or missed ball as a result of hitting on top of the ball. Proper timing will permit the ball to be struck as it appears to "hang" during the period when the ball is changing direction from ascent to descent or during the early stages of dropping while the ball is still well above the net. The ball should be struck with the heel of the hand, fingers carrying over the upper part of the ball, with the ball 1'-2' in front of the shoulder of the spiking arm. Striking at the ball with the fist will often result in a wild hit since the timing becomes even more critical. Striking with the fingers will usually result in an illegally handled ball.

A common fault in jumping for the spike is leaving the ground too soon. One must learn to time the jump so that you reach your maximum height at a time when the ball is just beginning its drop. Jumping too early will result in the predicament where the ball continues to move away from the spiker and stays just out of reach during ascent as well as descent. Approaching too soon will result in the spiker stopping to wait for the ball to descend to hitting position and therefore losing the momentum of the approach into the jump for the spike.

Rules of the Game 3

Rules governing play in volleyball have evolved throughout the years, since the origin of the game. As different groups played in various settings, rules were advanced to suit the individual situation.

Though an effort has been made to standardize play throughout the United States, there are several differing sets of rules in use, depending upon the affiliations of the group sponsoring the competition. In addition, the rules governing international competition have differed in minor respects from those which are in effect in amateur volleyball in the United States.

Currently most volleyball competition in the United States is played under the rules established by one of two rule-making bodies. The United States Volleyball Association has established rules which are in use in virtually all men's competition, whether on interscholastic, intercollegiate, or amateur level. All amateur women's competition, and most coeducational and recreational league play is also under the USVBA rules. The second rule-making body, the Division for Girls and Women's Sports of the American Association for Health, Physical Education and Recreation, publishes a set of rules used in most interscholastic and intercollegiate competition for women and girls.

In reality there is little difference in the actual playing of the games under the two sets of rules. The following sections are designed to give a summary of the USVBA rules, with exceptions noted where these occur according to DGWS rules. Rules, adaptions for doubles, beach volleyball and coeducational volleyball are given at the end of the chapter.

The Court, Net and Ball

The volleyball *court* playing surface measures thirty by sixty feet. It is bounded by lines two inches in width, and is divided into two identical square court areas by a four inch centerline. There should be at least a twenty-six foot *space above the court* free of obstructions. There should also be a minimum six-foot area beyond the rear of each court area, between an extension of the right sideline and a mark ten feet from the right sideline, known as the *service area*. If the minimum of six feet is not available, the serving area should be extended into the court the distance necessary to afford the server a six-foot area. (USVBA rules indicate that the center line is four inches wide, the total of two inches from either court. DGWS rules indicate that the center line is two inches wide.)

Additional lines are placed ten feet from each side of the center line and parallel to it. These lines are known as the *spiking lines* and govern the spiking area for back line players.

A *net,* measuring three feet by thirty-two feet, is tautly stretched from all four corners across the court over the center line. The height of the top of the net is eight feet from the floor for men's play and coeducational competition, and seven feet and four and one-quarter inches for women's play.

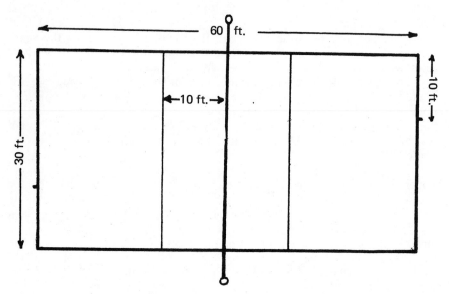

Figure 8–The Volleyball Court

The *volleyball* is twenty-seven inches in circumference and weighs approximately ten ounces. The outer casing, which should be laceless, is made of leather. The inflation of the ball should allow the ball to rebound vertically between sixty and sixty-five inches when dropped from a height of 100 inches to a concrete surface.

Teams, Players, Position and Substitutes

A volleyball *team* consists of six players positioned into a front line and a back line of three players each. At the time the ball is contacted on the service all players shall be positioned in serving order, and each front line player must be totally in front of each of his respective back-line player so that their feet in no way overlap. At the same time each

Are these men and women (M and W) in legal positions for receiving a serve?

player in both front and back line may not overlap laterally with the player to the right or the left in the same line. After the service all players may move to play or cover any area of the court with the stipulation that a back line player may not return the ball over the net from above net height while in advance of the ten foot line, and a back row player may not block.

Players must follow the *serving order* established with their positions at the start of the game. After the loss of service by the opponents, the serving team rotates one position in a clockwise direction.

Substitutions may be made upon request of and recognition by the official anytime the ball is dead. A player may enter the game three times, provided he enters each time at the same position relative to his teammates which he occupied at previous entries. Each team is limited to twelve substitutions per game. (Exception: DGWS—(1) a fifteen second time-out is taken to complete substitutions; and (2) only two entries per game are permitted, with no limitations on number of substitutions per team.)

Playing the Game

A *match* consists of three games. The team winning two out of three games is declared the winner. The *game* is played until eight minutes of actual playing time is concluded, or when one team has scored fifteen points, whichever occurs first. In either case the winning team must lead by two points before play is concluded. *Actual playing time* begins at the time the ball is put into play at each service, and the time the clock is stopped when the ball is dead after each play.

A *toss of the coin* determines which team will serve first and which court each team will occupy, the choice being given the winner of the toss and the loser receiving the alternate choice. Teams *change courts* after each game and at eight points or four minutes into the third game. The team not serving first in the first game serves first in the second game, and so on.

Three minutes is taken between games for rest and reorganization. Each team is permitted to call two team time-outs per game, the length of the time-out being thirty seconds. (Exception: DGWS—the length of team time-outs is one minute.)

The game is started with a service by the right back player on the serving team. The server is permitted to put the ball into play on each serve only after the referee has sounded his whistle. The player must be outside the court and within the service area until the ball is contacted on the serve. The ball may be hit or batted with the hand, fist, or arm, and is directed over the net between the side lines into the opponents' court. The server continues until his team loses the service or the game is completed. When one team loses the service its opponents will serve after having rotated one position clockwise. During the service it is illegal for a team to screen the server's action from the opponents' view in any way. If this occurs, side-out is called. It is also illegal to serve out of order. If the error is discovered during the service, all points scored during that service are deducted and the service is terminated. If, however, the error is not discovered until after the opponents have served after the illegal order, no penalty is assessed, but positions must be corrected. (Exception: DGWS—The receiving team on the first service of the game shall not rotate upon gaining the ball for its first service.)

After the service the ball must be *clearly hit* when it is volleyed by any player. It may be contacted with any part of the body above (and including) the waist, as long as a player does not play the ball twice in succession. If the ball contacts two parts of the body at the same time, this is considered to be one play. Simultaneous contact of the ball by teammates or by two opponents (above the net) constitutes one play, and either player may play the ball again. In addition, if a player participating in a block contacts the ball, he may play it again. Each team may play the ball only three times before it crosses the net to the opponents' court. A player may go outside the court to play the ball, provided that any ball hit over the net from out of bounds must cross the net over or between the sidelines.

When *playing at the net,* a player may not touch the net or its cable while the ball is in play. A player returning the ball may reach over the net to follow any otherwise legal play, as long as he first contacts the ball on his own side of the net. It is legal to reach over the net to block an opponent's hit, provided the opponent has hit the ball to return it. The ball may be played off the net. It is legal to touch the center line but illegal to touch beyond it into the opponents' court. It is also legal for a player to reach under the net to play a ball which is in play on his court, but it is illegal to reach under the net and interfere with opponents' activity. (Exception: DGWS—It is illegal to reach over the net to block a return.)

Conduct

It is considered to be unsportsmanlike to shout or stamp the feet while an opponent is in the act of playing the ball. Persistent comments to the official regarding decisions or making derogatory remarks to or about either officials or opponents also are considered to be gross misconduct and unsportsmanlike.

Fouls and Penalties

A *foul* is an infraction of the rules or a failure to play the ball properly. The penalty for fouls is a point scored for the opponents if the foul is committed by the receiving team, or side-out (loss of service) if the foul is committed by the serving team.

Fouls are called whenever (1) the server is out of the service area before the ball is contacted; (2) any player is illegally positioned on the service; (3) screening of the service is used; (4) a backline player, in attempting to spike, goes into the air in front of the ten foot line; (5) a player serves out of order; (6) the server fails to hit the ball clearly with hand, fist or arm; (7) the server hits the ball out of bounds, into the net, or fails to hit it completely over the net; (8) a player causes the ball to land out of bounds at any time during play; (9) a player does not clearly hit the ball (the ball may not visibly come to rest at the time it is contacted by the player); (10) one plays the ball successively (exception: after participating in a block or after having made a simultanous hit with either a teammate or an opponent, a player may play the ball again); (11) a team plays the ball more than three times before sending it to the opponents' court; (12) a substitute returns to the game in a position other than his orginal one, in relation to his teammates; (13) a server unnecessarily delays putting the ball into play; (14) a player touches the net, reaches over the net, crosses the center line, or interferes with opponents under the net, while the ball is in play (exception: a blocker may reach over the net to block a return provided the opponent has hit the ball; (15) a player enters the game more than three times or otherwise substitutes illegally; (16) a player delays the game in any unnecessary manner; (17) a team calls more than two time-outs per game. (Exception: DGWS—a player may enter a game only two times.)

If unsportsmanlike conduct occurs, the official may invoke the penalty for the foul or at his discretion may disqualify the player from the game.

If two opponents commit fouls simultaneously, a double foul is called and the point is replayed.

Several other violations of rules may occur during play. These are summarized as follows: (1) a time-out is charged to a team which fails to substitute without delay; (2) a player entering the game for the fourth time or in the wrong position must leave the game; (3) all points scored are cancelled if made by an improper server or while an illegally entered or positioned re-entry player is on the court. (4) a forfeit game, scoring 15-0 is called if a team does not have six players or refuses to begin play. (Exception: DGWS—(1) a team time-out is assessed a team which takes longer than fifteen seconds to complete a substitution; (2) a player making a third entry must leave the game; and (3) no concellation of points is called for when illegally entered players are on court.)

A *point is replayed* whenever (1) an official commits an error; (2) any object enters the court or there is interference with play; (13) a player serves the ball before the official's whistle signals for service; (4) a player is injured and a time-out is called while the ball is in play; (5) a double foul occurs.

Coeducational Rules

All rules given above apply to coeducational play except: (1) the serving order shall alternate one man and one woman throughout the line-up (2) when the ball is played by more than one player on a side, one hit shall be made by a woman before the ball is returned to the opponents: (3) the net shall be 8 feet in height; and (4) when one male player is in the front row one back row player may come to the net to block.

Doubles Rules

All rules given above apply to doubles play except: (1) each team's court measure thirty feet wide and twenty-five feet deep; (2) no substitutes are permitted; (the serve must come from the right half of the rear court area; (4) a game consists of eleven points or five minutes actual playing time.

Beach Rules

All rules given prior to the foregoing sections apply except (1) the net is placed seven feet and ten inches above hard packed sand, and seven feet and nine inches above loosely packed sand; (2) teams change courts after each five points are scored; (3) ropes are used as boundaries; (4) contact with the center rope is a foul, but if a player's foot is under the rope without contacting it, no foul is called.

Officials and their Duties

For the purpose of controlling play in a manner equitable to each team, the following officials are used: a referee, an umpire, a timekeeper, a scorekeeper, and two to four linesmen.

The *referee*, the official in charge, is stationed in an elevated position at one end of the net and makes decisions on all playing of the ball, declares point and side-out, and may at anytime overrule another official if he feels an error has occurred. The referee shall confer with and instruct all the other officials with reference to their duties. The referee indicates that play shall start on each service with a whistle. The whistle is blown to indicate that any infraction of the rules has occurred during play. The referee should use appropriate signals to indicate his calls. *Signals* include: (1) point—hand nearest team scoring raised with forefinger extended; (2) side-out—hand nearest team to gain the service is extended toward that team with hand open, palm upward; (3) over the net—hand extended over the net from side of the infraction; (4) touching the net—touch the net on the side of the infraction; (5) crossing center line—hand extended under net from side of infraction; (6) thrown ball—hand and forearm make throwing motion; (7) lifting the ball—underhand lifting motion upward; (8) held ball—both hands in volleying position with motion of closing fingers, then opening fingers; (9) time-out—hands form a T on side of team requesting time-out; (10) substitution—hands are rotated around one another in front of body.

The *umpire,* stationed at the opposite end of the net from the referee, assists in calling violations regarding positioning, conduct, substitution, and interference with play, as well as makes decisions in regard to net and center line fouls. The umpire uses the same signals as the referee whenever appropriate.

The *scorer,* seated near the umpire's position, is charged with keeping an accurate account of the score and all other recorded information, and informing the referee or umpire of violations or fouls committed by either team relative to substitution, positioning, or time-outs.

The *timekeeper* is also near the umpire and scorer and handles all timing devices, accurately recording the actual playing time and time used for time-outs.

Linesmen are positioned at the rear corners of the court to assist in indicating whether balls are in or out of court. The linesman should have a small flag in hand, indicating "out" by raising the hand with flag, and indicating "in" by pointing the flag downward. Linesmen also assist in watching to see that the server remains in the serving area and that a ball crossing the net from out of bounds crosses between the net markers for the sideline. They also assist in retrieving the ball when time-outs are called. If two linesmen are used, each is positioned at the left rear corners and is responsible for the rear court line and the sideline on his side of the court. If four linesmen are used, the rear court linesmen are positioned on the right rear corners, and the side linesmen are positioned on the left rear court corners.

4 Patterns of Play

Team play is *essential* in volleyball. The effectiveness of any team is directly related to the coordination of the abilities and responsibilities of its members. Outstanding spiking does not occur without precison setting. The setter's ability to place the ball for the spiker depends largely upon the ability of the team's members to control the ball on the first volley as it comes from the opponents' court. The possibility of controlling the first hit is dependent upon a well coordinated defense. Each player must do his best to enhance the team's play.

Each game situation places new and different demands upon each player in each postiion on the court. Successful teamwork requires that a player know all the team patterns which have been established, think quickly and anticipate situations before they arise, and make a maximum effort to carry out his responsibilities.

The sections which follow are designed to present concepts of offense and defense in volleyball. The first section, *Basic Concepts of Strategy and Team Play,* covers the fundamentals of team play which the beginning player and team should follow, and upon which most intermediate and advanced strategy concepts are based. The second section, *Intermediate Offensive and Defensive Concepts,* covers these aspects in depth and should be useful for players and teams who have begun to master the fundamental techniques of the game. *Advanced Offensive and Defensive Concepts* are briefly surveyed in section three to acquaint the reader with the potential of strategy for the game of volleyball. The final section is devoted to some approaches to strategy in *Coeducational Volleyball.*

Basic Concepts of Strategy and Team Play

Basic Pass Pattern. The spike is the key offensive weapon in volleyball. To insure opportunities for the spike, a general pass pattern is used. As the ball comes over the net from the opponents' court, whether on a serve or a rally return, an attempt should be made to *pass* (1) the ball to the setter, usually the center front player. The setter then *sets* (2) the ball to either the left front or right front player for the *spike.* (3) The *pass-set-spike* pattern is the basis for volleyball offense. (Figure 9)

The right and left front positions are considered to be the fundamental spiker's positions because the distances to the farthest boundaries of the opponents' court are generally longer from these positions than from the center front. This affords a spiker a choice of angles for the spike with the assurance of the greatest possibility of keeping the ball within the court boundaries. Figure 10 illustrates these angles with solid line arrows. The center spiking angles are shown in figure 10 with dotted line arrows. It can be readily seen that angles available to the center spiker result in generally shorter distances than those available to the left or right front spiker. The center hit is a planned strategy at advanced levels of play when spikers have the skill capabilities of placing the spike with the high degree of accuracy demanded.

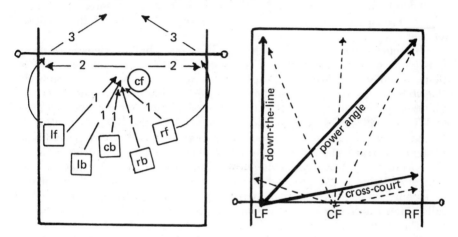

Figure 9—Pass-Set-Spike Pattern   *Figure 10—Spiking Angles*

Assuming that all the spikers on a team are right handed, the left front position is known as the *on-hand* spiking position. This term is used because the spiker's hitting arm is on the same side as the direction of the approaching set. Conversely, the right front position is called the *off-hand* side because the set must cross the spiker's body to be in position for the spiking hand. For lefthanded spikers the left front position is the off-hand, and the right front position is the on-hand side.

The first hit on the side, or the *pass,* is normally executed with the forearm pass. The pass should be directed toward the center front area of the court to a height of about 5 to 8 feet above net height. This height of arc is necessary to give the setter time to get into position to make a good set. The pass should be placed in front of the setter as the setter faces the sideline. This is preferred to a pass directly overhead or behind the setter so that the setter is able to move forward to execute the play.

The *set* should be placed in a position from which the spiker can attack the ball. A regular set is placed 1½ to 2 feet from the net and about 5 feet above net height. The set should be placed wide, toward the sideline, so that the spiker will approach the ball from slightly outside the court and contact the ball just inside the sideline. Wide sets are desirable since this allows longer spiking angles, and forces the defense to cover the full thirty foot width of the court and net.

The setter must move quickly to the pass and should make every attempt to squarely face the direction of the desired set. The setter should feel obligated to get to the ball if the pass is placed anywhere near the center front of the court. He should attempt to move constantly with one side to the net rather than turning his back to the net to watch the passer. With his side to the net the setter can turn the head to watch the ball and sliding steps can be taken to the ball while facing the direction of the desired set. Moving to the ball with the back to the net forces the setter to accomplish between a 90 and 180 degree turn to face the position for the set.

Inaccurate passing occurs at all levels of play, but happens most often at beginning levels. Therefore, a team should have some simple alternate plans to carry out the pass-set-spike patterns. If the pass is inaccurately placed into the air and approaches the left or right front positions, the player in that position should call the setter away from the play ("mine" or "I've got it") and execute a *cross-court set* to the opposite spiker. If the pass remains in the back court, the available back court player who is facing forward should call the setter away from the play and should place a *back-court set* to the diagonally opposite spiker. The diagonal set is recommended in preference to a set to the spiker directly in front of the back-court player because a diagonal set is much easier to spike than a ball which approaches directly from behind.

The *spike* is described in detail in Chapter 2. At beginning levels, however, the spiker often finds it difficult to position properly for the approach to the spike. Often a pass and set occur only to find the spiker standing at the net, unable to approach for the spike and often out of position to make even a jump in place for the spike. Each player who is either in the left or right front position must *think like a spiker*. As the ball is passed on the first hit, if the spiker is not needed to assist as a setter, he should retreat immediately to about 10 feet from the net and on or outside the sideline to await the set. If the pass comes between the spiker and the setter, the spiker should let the setter take it so that the spiker can be available to spike. If the ball comes over the net in such a way that either setter or spiker could make the pass (first hit), the spiker should take the ball and pass to the setter who will in turn set for the spiker.

It is often necessary to *play an inaccurate set* over the net. There are several alternatives when the set is so off-target that the spike is not possible. The one hand top-spin hit can be used if the player is able to face the net behind the ball to hit the ball overhead. This is a spike-type hitting action which places the ball to deep court areas with a good deal of force. The player positions himself so that the ball is at full arm's reach overhead and 10 to 15 inches in front of the hitting shoulder. By hitting from below the center of gravity of the ball with sharp upward pressure the desired top-spin is gained. The farther the ball is from the net, the lower on the ball is the contact point required to gain the proper trajectory for the ball to cross the net.

If the pass and set are so poorly controlled that the third hit will be played from out of bounds, from deep court, or from an off-balance position, the forearm pass should be used to play the ball over the net. The basic objective is to get the ball over the net and to keep the ball in play. The player making this play should turn the side to the net, take a wide stride position, drawing the arms (positioned for the forearm pass) back with the rear arm and shoulder higher than the forward arm and shoulder. The ball is stroked with the forward motion of the arms and a forceful weight shift to the forward foot. The side to the net position is recommended in preference to a back to the net position so that the player can have a better perspective of the angle and flight needed to place the ball over the net into the opponents' court.

Receiving Service. The server who can place the serve or who can create deceptive floating or spinning action of the ball is on the offensive. This makes the receiving of the service a defensive maneuver. The serve must be handled and controlled before the receiving team can assume the offensive. Careful observation by experienced teams and coaches has indicated that the majority of serves in most volleyball games fall into the middle third of the receiving team's court. For good coverage, then, the receiving team should flood this center court area with each player aware of the area for which he has responsibility. If the individual server serves consistently deep or short the entire team alignment can make minor adjustments to cover these circumstances.

Figure 11 shows the recommended alignment for receiving service. The center front player is near the net to be out of the receiving formation and to be available to make the set. The setter is off-set to the right so that any one of the receiving players can more easily pass the ball in front of

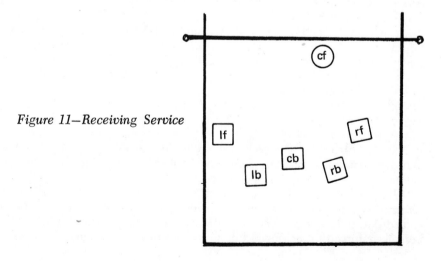

Figure 11—Receiving Service

When a switch is desired, what error in receiving the serve is being made in this 4-2 arrangement?

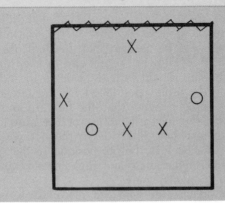

the setter as the setter faces the on-hand spiker. All five receivers are turned to face the server who must serve from the right rear one-third of the opposite court. Because the server is restricted to serving from the right ten-foot area of his rear court, the receiving alignment is pulled to their left, since it will be virtually impossible for the server to place the ball over the net to the right hand sideline in the front half of the court. The left front, center back and right front players are responsible for receiving any ball which is below waist level in front of, and to the right and left of their starting positions. The left back and right back players are responsible for balls directly in front of them and any ball above waist level for the front line players. The left back takes all balls behind the left front and over the left shoulder of the center back. The right back takes any ball over the center back player's head and right shoulder and beyond the reach of the right front player. In addition, the right and left back players should back up one another.

Each member of the receiving team should take a *stance* which will permit him to move quickly in any direction. It is suggested that all players take a balanced stance with one foot slightly ahead of the other, and with the knees flexed. The hands should be carried about waist high. This is called the "ready position."

Players should be certain to *avoid overlapping positions* when receiving service. It is illegal to overlap with players on either side in the same row or to overlap with the player directly in front or in back of the player in the official line-up positions. For example, the left front and left back may not overlap, the center front and center back may not overlap, and so on.

Defensive Positioning and Movement. When awaiting the ball to be returned by the opponents, the team must be defensively ready. The returned ball will normally move in one of two flight patterns. It will either be spiked forcefully downward or it will be played over in a more lofted arc and with less force. This indicates the necessity for the defensive team to be prepared for either alternative and requires two different choices in defensive positioning to adequately cover the court.

The lofted arc return can be fielded with the forearm pass and converted immediately into the pass-set-spike offense. It becomes evident, however, as opponents develop power and control in the spike that the court average to field the spike is increasingly difficult. A well-formed block at the net is required to divert the intentions of the spiker for sound defense.

There are numerous defensive systems used in volleyball. The system suggested in this section is considered to be easily mastered by beginners and one which will most adequately cover the majority of returns that occur in beginning levels of play, namely, the half-speed spike or a "save" play return with a forearm pass. This defense is known as the *center back up* or "dink" defense.

Figure 12 shows the *base position* for the center-back-up defense. This position should be taken at the time of one's own team's service or at anytime the ball is returned to the opponents. From this position either the block or the no block defense option can be assumed. Since the *block defense* must develop more quickly the base position anticipates the spike. In the base position all front row players face the net, standing about 18 inches from it with hand up at shoulder height. The center back player positions at about midcourt, while the left and right back players position 4-5 feet from the rear lines and 2-3 feet from the sidelines.

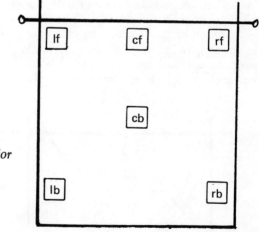

Figure 12—Base Position for Center-Back-Up Defense

The *no block defense* is used whenever it is anticipated that the opposing spiker cannot execute a hard spike. This defense is used whenever the return is from mid-court or rear-court, when a set to a spiker is inaccurate so that the spiker is off-balance or poorly positioned, or when the spiker is known to be unable to forcefully spike the ball downward. The player who would normally set the block calls "no block" and the position shown in figure 13 is assumed.

The diagram for the *no block defense* shows the position if the ball is returned from the opponents' left front. It should be noted that the center front player, the setter, has stayed near the net out of the way of play so that he may be available to set the ball from the pass. All other players have positioned themselves almost identical to the serve reception "W" formation, with the exception that the formation is turned and adjusted to face the direction of the anticipated return while covering the possible angles of flight for that return. If the return were to be from the center or right side of the opponents' court comparable adjustments to face the direction of the net and coverage of angles would be made.

The effectiveness of a *blocking defense* is dependant upon good blocking mechanics and teamwork. Prior to blocking, the defensive team takes the *base position* shown in figure 12. As the ball comes to the opponents' setter, all front row players are within 12 to 18 inches from the net, with vision focused on the ball. As the setter places the ball for the spiker, the blocker directly opposite the spiker assumes the placement of the block directly in front of the ball. Meanwhile the center blocker turns and runs with several long strides toward the side blocker. The two-player block is formed as the center blocker plants the foot nearest the side blocker and pivots toward the net with knees bent and weight low ready to jump for the block. As the center blocker approaches, the side blocker crouches with hands in a ready position to thrust upward. (Figure 14) The center blocker makes arm or shoulder contact with the side blocker and the jump for the block is coordinated so that there is no more than three to four inches between all of the blocking hands. The hand nearest the sideline is turned in toward the court to contain the spike. The blockers' hands may reach over the net, as long as the spiker is allowed to first contact the ball. The blockers should absorb the force of the recovery to the court by landing

Figure 13—"No Block" Defense

Figure 14—Forming the Block

on the balls of the feet and flexing the knees and ankles. The hands and arms should be retracted with control to avoid net fouls.

As shown in figure 15, as the block is formed, the player at the net who is away from the direction of the set falls away from the net when he sees the set placed, in order to assist in covering the remaining area of

Figure 15—Covering the Block (Center-Back-Up)

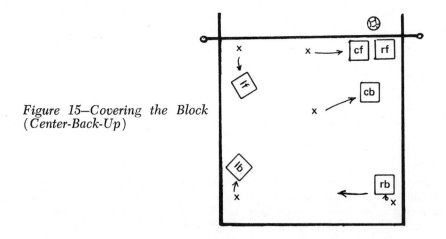

the court. As the set is made to the spiker, all nonblocking defensive players are deployed to cover all angles of potential returns past or over the block. The left front and the center back players must be prepared to pick up all soft drop volleys, or "dinks," over and to the sides of the block as well as partially blocked shots which are deflected into the short court area. In addition, the left front player shares responsibility with the left back player in fielding all spiked balls angled past the block. The left back player positions just to the left of the left shoulder of the center blocker.

If the block is set as described above it should prevent shots down the near sideline. (The various concepts of block placement are presented in the next section.) The right back player, therefore, is responsible to move to any balls which are hit off the blocker's hands or which are hit over the block. In addition, he should be alert to move to cover the appropriate angle should he see that either blocker will be late to the block or will be slow jumping.

Covering the Spiker. The well-executed spike will be "put away" to win a rally at beginning levels of play. As the opponents gain experience in the use of the blocking defense, the offensive team must be alert to react to blocked returns. If the block is successful, the ball may rebound to the spiker's side of the net. Very often the blocked ball will drop over the spiker to the area on the court just behind him. It is necessary for the spiker's teammates to be ready to cover this possibility and to try to reset for another spike and regain the offensive.

The diagram, figure 16, indicates the movement of the spiker's teammates when the ball is set to the left front player. All players should be

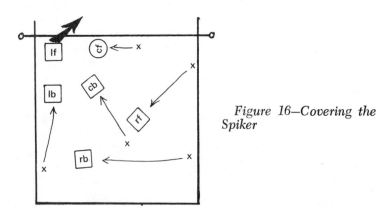

Figure 16—Covering the Spiker

alert, in a ready position with the hands carried at waist level. The left back, center back and center front players move in quickly to cover the short block with a semi-circle formation behind the spiker. The right back swings to the left to cover the deep block to the left back area, and the right front moves back to cover the center and right deep court area.

Intermediate Offensive and Defensive Concepts

Once the basic team strategies are understood and the fundamental skills are mastered, several additional approaches to offense and defense will enhance the excitement of the game. In most instances the tactics offered in this section are built upon an understanding of the basic concepts outlined in the preceding section.

Four-Two Offensive System. As experience with the game increases it becomes obvious that some players are more effective than others as spikers while some are more valuable as setters. The 4-2 offense is designed to take advantage of the specific strengths of individual players by aligning four spikers and two setters on the court so that there are always one setter and two spikers in the front row. When a spiker rotates to the center front, the setter in the front row *exchanges position* with that spiker by legally *switching* to the center front position.

Figure 17 shows the *receive of service* positions when the setters are center front and center back, and no switching is required. After one rotation from the original position, the alignment shown in figure 18 will be taken to receive the serve. The five player reception formation is identical to that in figure 17, except that the center front (spiker) has moved to the position previously taken by the right front. The right front setter moves to the extreme right area near the net, and as soon as the serve is contacted, moves into the center front area to set. The center front spiker functions from the right front position. All players involved in switching must hold position until the serve is contacted so that overlapping does

Figure 17—Receiving Service—4-2 Offense

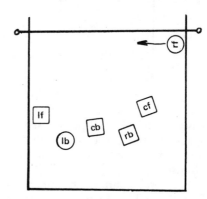

Figure 18—Receiving Service—4-2 Offense With Setter's Switch

not occur. This includes not only the center front and right front players, but also the position of the center back player in relation to the center front player. Since the center front player has pulled back to assist in receiving serve, he must be certain to be positioned nearer the net than the center back player.

When the team rotates another position, it will be noted from figure 19, the right front setter will move to the back row and the left back setter will move to the front row in the left front position. When the setter is in the left front for reception of service, he positions near the net and as near the sideline as possible, while the center front player pulls back to cover the left front receiving position. After the ball is contacted on the service the setter moves to the center front area and the center front player functions as the left front spiker. It must be remembered that if a switch has occurred, all players must return to original positions prior to each service .

The *switch for the serving team* is always much easier than for the receiving team since the ball must be returned before the ball is to be played. Figure 19 illustrates the left front setter and center front spiker switch. The two players position near one another and after the ball is contacted on the service each player moves to the base position for defense at the net.

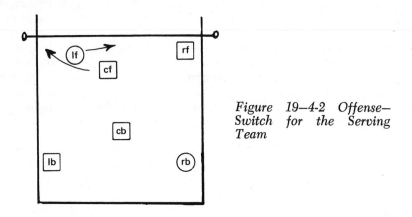

Figure 19–4-2 Offense– Switch for the Serving Team

Service Tactics. The most important factor in maintaining an offensive advantage is a well-placed service. If the serve falls into the uncovered spaces of the court the result is an immediate score. If the serve results in passing errors, the receiving team will be less able to develop a potent offense.

Several court areas are vulnerable in the traditional serve reception formation. The deep side lines areas are very vulnerable. If the serve is executed with either floating or spinning action, the resultant pass is often played toward the out-of-bounds area where there is no one readily available to play the next hit.

The deep center back court area is also vulnerable in that it causes the left and right back players to coordinate the coverage. If either player hesitates, the serve may fall in for a point, or the pass may be poorly placed. Short serves which clear the net within 2 to 3 feet from net height and are placed to the areas between the right front and center back, or between the center back and the left front often create handling errors for the receiving team. The short serve has a very small margin of error, but the server who has mastered control of it through practice has a decided advantage.

Another aspect of vulnerability can be discovered in an analysis of the passing abilities of the receiving team players. Serves placed to the weaker passers can result in costly passing errors.

Finally, consideration of the position of the receiving team's strongest spikers is important. A serve placed to the side of the court away from the strongest spiker in the front row will cause the pass to be taken by the setter so that a less reliable back set must be ultilized to get the set to that strong spiker.

Setting Tactics. Setting is the key to sound offensive volleyball. The setter who keeps track of all the game circumstances may often create an advantage for the offense by advantageously placing the ball for the spiker.

The setter should have a good knowledge of the spikers on his own team with regard to abilities as well as desires in types of sets, and should attempt to adjust sets accordingly.

It is also imperative that the setter know the opposing team. The attempt should be made to set away from the opponents' strongest blockers, while setting to the opponents' blocking weaknesses.

The competent setter will work to develop basic technique in setting which will not tip off the direction or type of set to the opposing team. This is vital in fooling the block. The effective setter will also seek to move the sets to both sides of the court, using maximum court width so that the blockers will be forced to move rapidly to cover the play.

When the setter is off-balance due to a bad pass the attempt should be made to set to the easiest position possible, which is usually a front set. If the spiker has been placed off-balance or has been slow in the spike approach due to fatigue, the setter should set the ball slightly higher than usual to assist the spiker in timing the approach.

Spike Variations. At beginning and early intermediate stages of learning to spike the player will see nothing but the ball and the net during the approach and jump to spike. With experience, however, the spiker should begin utilizing peripheral vision to see the position of the blockers and take advantage by placing the spike at the appropriate angles past the block or through the holes in the block. This technique is known as "reading the block."

In addition, the thinking spiker will check the defense prior to each service to see how the blockers have positioned in the front row so that a slow moving blocker, a short blocker or a poor jumping blocker can be spotted. The backcourt defense should also be kept in mind so that the ball can be placed to an open space.

The effective spiker will have full command of the spike and should be able to choose the angle of the spike at the latest possible moment. The spiker should always be prepared to dink the ball to an open space or hit a half-speed spike to catch the defense off balance. These tactics are especially deceiving when used by a strong spiker, because the defense cannot adequately cover all the alternatives of his potential actions.

Finally, the spiker who is developing in ability should work to use the blockers' hands to win points. A spike placed to hit off the outside hand of the side line blocker will usually rebound out of bounds out of reach of the defense.

Line-up Considerations. The line-up is established with thought given to both offensive and defensive abilities of players. The type of offense used will also dictate certain factors. With the 4-2 offense the following factors are usually considered.

With two spikers and one setter in the front row at all times, usually the strongest spiker starts in the left front, with the second strongest spiker starting in the right back position. This assures the team of having one strong spiker in the front row at all times. The other two spikers are placed in relation to their respective serving and defensive abilities.

The first two or three servers in the line-up should possess strong serves. The strongest blockers should start left back, left front and center front, while the players starting right front, right back and center back should be strong in backcourt defense since these are the positions in the line-up which will usually be confronted with the opponents' strongest attack.

In the 4-2 offense the setters can be started either in the center positions or at either of the side positions. If the spiker is especially effective on the on-hand side that spiker should lead the adjacent setter in the line-up since this will switch that spiker to the on-hand side when the spiker is center front.

Blocking Tactics. The placement of the block is critical to a soundly functioning defense. There are two basic placements. In the first, the block is set to *give the line* to the spiker. This means that the block will be established to take away the majority of the wider cross court angle space, and invite the spiker to hit to the much narrower area between the block and the sideline. This can be seen in figure 20. This tactic is very effective

Figure 20 – Giving the Line

against the beginning spiker since he often cannot adequately place the hit down the sideline at will, and will almost invariably spike cross court into the block.

The second block placement is that of *taking the line*. This can be seen in figure 21. This block is designed to force all spikes into the cross court angle. Usually this block placement is accompanied by strong back-court coverage into the cross court area past the block to field the spikes which are not contained by the block.

Figure 21—Taking the Line

The *attack block* is an offensive use of the block. It requires that the blockers be able to jump well and have good body control. As the block is formed the blockers reach the hands and forearms well over the net in an umbrella-like position over the spike, meeting the ball with the firm forward thrust before retracting the hands and returning to the court. The result is a spiked ball which is blocked forcefully down to the court with little chance of the spiker's teammates retrieving it.

Center-back-deep Defense. In the first section of the chapter (p. 25-27) a team defense is presented which is strong in coverage of the spike, soft hits and dinks, but which is vulnerable in the deep center back area of the court. An alternate defense is the center-back-deep defense which is strong in blocking the spike and in deep back court coverage, but somewhat vulnerable to the dink. The choice in defenses depends on the strengths of the opponents.

The base position for this defense is shown in figure 22. It will be noted that all base positions are identical to those in figure 12 except for the center back player who starts in the back line in the middle of the court.

Figure 23 illustrates the blocking of a spike from the opposing left front. As the block is set the left front pulls away from the net and is alert to field the acutely angled shot past the block or a soft hit short to the center of the court. The left back positions just outside the left shoulder of the center blocker to field the hard hit spikes past the block. The center back player takes a position on a line from the ball to the spot between the two blockers. He is responsible for all balls rebounding off the block deep to the back court or any ball, hit over or through the block. The right back player covers the line. If the block "gives the line" this player must hold position until it can be seen whether or not the spiker will hit to the line. If the block "takes the line" this player can charge forward to cover behind the block for dinks and soft deflections off the block.

Defensive Switching. It is possible to make interchanges of position on the court after the service to better deploy defensive players to take

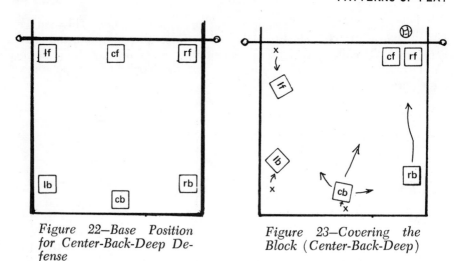

Figure 22—Base Position for Center-Back-Deep Defense

Figure 23—Covering the Block (Center-Back-Deep)

advantage of specific defensive abilities. These switches are quite simple when executed by the serving team. When executed by the receiving team these switches are usually done as the players move from the cover of their own spiker into their base positions for defense. Only the most necessary switches should be attempted after receiving service and spiking, since confusion can easily occur and disrupt the offense.

Advanced Offensive and Defensive Concepts

Numerous teams competing at the advanced level of play do so using the basic and intermediate tactics described in the preceding sections. The difference between intermediate and advanced play often is the consistently excellent performance of the fundamental skills and tactics by the advanced level player. In addition to excellence in performance, some advanced teams use more intricate offenses than those outlined above. These offenses demand some countering defensive considerations.

Multiple Offense. The multiple offense utilizes all three front row players as spikers. The setter is a back row player who moves into the right front area, about ten feet in from the right sideline, and chooses to front set to either of two on-hand spikers (left front or center front), or back set to the off-hand spiker (right front). The fact that the offense now has three potential spikers, coupled with the deceptive setting variations and decoying movements by the spikers, creates many problems for the defensive team.

There are three different team approaches to the multiple offense—the 5-1, 6-0 and 6-2 offenses. The *5-1 offense* is one in which the team has five spikers and one setter. The setter starts in the right back position as shown in figure 24. As the ball is contacted by the server the setter runs into the right front passing area. Figure 25 illustrates the movement when the setter has rotated to the center back. When the setter becomes the left back, the movement to the right side passing area is difficult, so an alternate choice would be to set from the left front area with the setter facing two off-hand spikers as shown in figure 26. As the setter rotates to the front row the offense becomes identical to a 4-2 offense with the setter switching into the center front. This 4-2 type offense continues until the setter again rotates into the right back position.

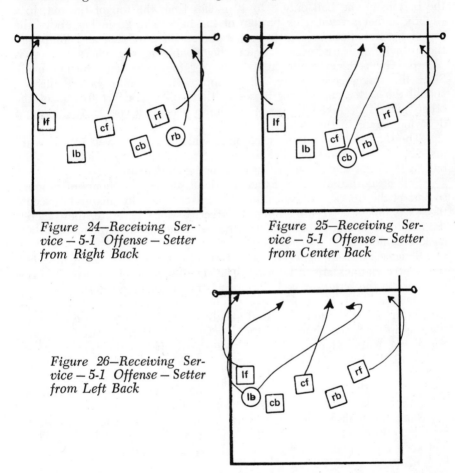

Figure 24—Receiving Service — 5-1 Offense — Setter from Right Back

Figure 25—Receiving Service — 5-1 Offense — Setter from Center Back

Figure 26—Receiving Service — 5-1 Offense — Setter from Left Back

The *6-0 offense* is based on the multiple attack of three spikers in the front row, but demands that each spiker also be a capable setter. Each spiker, upon reaching the right back position, runs into the front row as a setter as shown in figure 24.

In the *6-2 offense* the team is composed of four spikers and two setter-spikers. The setter-spikers start opposite one another, and when in the back row function as a setter, but upon reaching the front row function as a spiker.

Setting Variations for Multiple Offense. The regular set described in preceding sections is used in the multiple offense, but is accompanied by other set variations which are designed to deceive the blockers.

When the setter receives a good pass he has the option of setting a short front set to the center front player or a short back set to the right front player. The short set can vary from an extremely low set placed with the bottom of the ball only 8 to 10 inches from the top of the net, to a slightly higher set with the bottom of the ball 15 to 20 inches above the top of the net. Both sets require that the spiker approach and jump into the air with the arm cocked before being able to see where the set is placed. The setter virtually places the set to the spiker's hitting hand. Since the spiker commits himself to approach and jump before the set, should the setter choose not to set to that spiker and set to one of the other spikers, the faked approach and jump become a very distracting and decoying factor to the defense.

The *shoot set* is another variation in which the set travels in a low arc just above and almost parallel to the net tape. The spiker intercepts the ball in its flight and drives it into the opponents' court.

Spiking both the short set and the shoot set requires hours of practice to perfect the timing and execution. The setter is usually unable to execute these sets unless he receives almost perfect passing, therefore, these tactics are not recommended for use until the team members have mastered the basic techniques.

Signals are used between the spiker and the setter to indicate when these set variations are to be used. The signal can be given visually prior to a pass to the setter, or verbally during the pass to the setter.

Defense Against the Multiple Offense. The basic team defenses described in earlier sections are used at advanced levels also. To counter-act the multiple offense, however, the blockers are often required to block one-on-one if the offense is extremely deceptive. If the direction of the set can be read, a two player block can be formed. To counter-act the center spike a one or two player block can be formed, depending on the spiking tendencies of the hitter, while the remaining defensive players attempt to cover the backcourt area at angles past the block.

Since the multiple offense setting variations require excellent passing, one of the best defenses against them is a strong offense and serve. These will keep the opponents off-balance while passing and therefore less able to generate a strong offense.

Transition from Offense to Defense. The setter who has run into the front row from the back row may not participate in the block. After the offense has returned the ball to the opponents the setter returns to the back row. In order that this transition be made smoothly, the setter always moves to a prearranged position depending on the defense employed by his team. If the center-back-deep defense is used the setter switches into the right back position. If the center-back-up defense is used the setter becomes the player under the block, or the center back. From these positions the movement back and forth from offense to defense is simplified.

Coeducational Volleyball

Coeducational play presents slightly different strategy problems than those encountered in men's or women's volleyball. Usually the men attempt to absorb the power aspects of the game. Therefore the men form the basic receiving formation on the service and form a two player block on defense with the third man in position to field the hard hit ball past the block. The women function as setters, and on defense cover the block and the court angles to field the softer placement shots and balls which are deflected by the block. Since the net is eight feet high the women are rarely used as spikers.

Receiving Service and Offense. The diagrams in figure 27 and 28 show the serve reception formations for the two situations in co-ed play. With two men in the front row the pass is made to the woman in the center front who is the setter, while the spikers hit from the left and right front areas. With one man in the front row the spiker may choose to hit from the center or may swing to the right or left front areas, depending on the direction of the pass. Either front row woman is the setter.

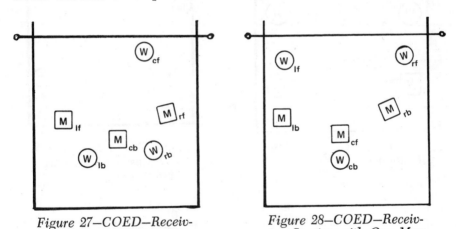

Figure 27—COED—Receiv-
ing Service with Two Men
in Front Row

Figure 28—COED—Receiv-
ing Service with One Man
in Front Row

Defense Against the Spike. Defense for strong spiking in mixed volleyball presents some interesting problems. Not only do the men absorb the power aspects of the game, but they must often block after moving great distances to get in position to do so. In addition, the strategy demands a great deal of switching of the men and women. The reader is encouraged to carefully study the diagrams so that the switches can be noted. Care must also be taken to avoid overlapping.

The defense presented here is one of several which could be employed. This defense is built on the concept that a two man block is always used. The block is always placed so that it *takes the line* (figure 21) *on the opponent's on-hand side* (block at own right front), and that the block always *gives the line* (Figure 20) *on the opponent's off-hand side* (block at own left front). With this positioning the third man (not blocking) is always positioned in the left back area. From there he fields the hard hits on the crosscourt angles from the opponent's on-hand, and the hard hits down the line on the opponent's off-hand.

The base position for this defense is shown in figure 29. The actual positions of player for the defense depends upon the rotation. With two men in the front row, figure 30 shows the position at service with the arrows indicating the movement to the base positions. Figures 31 and 32 indicate the block and coverage for the spike at the opponent's on-hand and off-hand sides, respectively.

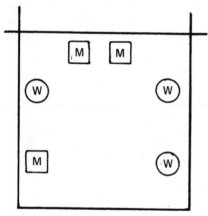

Figure 29 — COED — Base Position for Defense

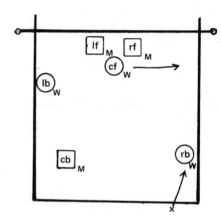

Figure 30—COED—Switch for Defense with Two Men in Front Row

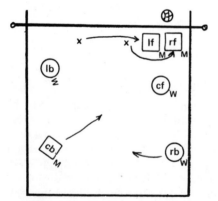

Figure 31—COED—Block for Opponents' On-hand Spike with Two Men in Front Row

Figure 32—COED—Block for Opponents' Off-hand Spike with One Man in Front Row

With the rotation placing one man in the front row, the same base position is taken on defense, but players come from different positions than shown here. Figure 33 shows the position at the time for service with arrows indicating the movement to the base positions. Figures 34 and 35 show the block and coverage of the back court for the opponent's on-hand and off-hand spikes, respectively.

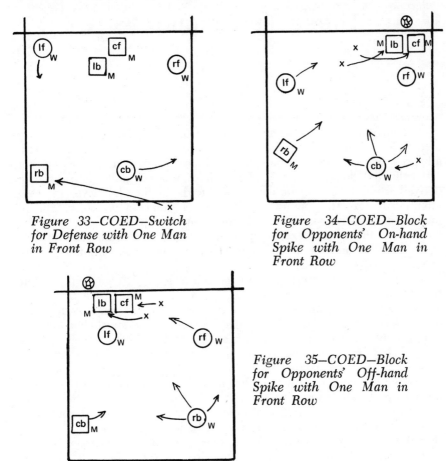

Figure 33—COED—Switch for Defense with One Man in Front Row

Figure 34—COED—Block for Opponents' On-hand Spike with One Man in Front Row

Figure 35—COED—Block for Opponents' Off-hand Spike with One Man in Front Row

The Spirit of Team Play

If a team is to be successful it is necessary for all members to play the game to the limits of their abilities. The thrill of a good performance can be experienced again and again by the player who is mentally alert, and who will make every possible effort to carry out his assignments. An even greater thrill is in store for the player who will seek, through his own play, to enhance the performance of his teammate. Complete confidence in, and respect for one's teammate is the basis of real team play.

5 Better Players Master These Techniques

Volleyball has been identified as the most popular participant sport in America. It should be recognized, however, that this statement includes all levels of play and varieties of conditions. Enjoyment is possible with rather limited skills but as the players improve their skills the satisfaction derived from the game increases many-fold. As the skill level increases, attention to the "fine points" of the game becomes a necessity. The following material is presented with the thought that while beginners may have some difficulty in executing advanced movement skills effectively, it is necessary to understand them in order to make them ultimately a part of your game.

Probably the most critical skill for you to learn is "court sense." Court sense is the ability to be in the right place at the right time by reacting to your opponent's game so that you are always in good position for either offensive or defensive play. Better players continually adjust their positions during play even when they do not appear to be directly involved in the action. They are always ready for the unexpected. They are actually calculating the probability that the opponent will follow a predictable course of action. As more information develops the player predicts the options for the spiker and moves to a position which will optimize the chances for fielding the ball. A spiker, on the other hand, develops the ability to "read the block." This advanced skill will determine whether the spiker should hit crosscourt, down the line, over the block or even use a "dink" that will drop the ball just behind the blockers. The ability to make this last second decision marks the advanced player.

The development of court sense is speeded up if you get into the habit of determining how you can position yourself on each play in order to be most effective. Think about the elements of the game. Ask yourself, "Was I in the best possible position during the rally?" Remember that these automatic adjustments require constant attention to the details of the action of play.

Another advanced skill is "digging" with one hand. Most beginners after a little experience begin to field the ball while moving. The next step is to learn to move so that you can get the forearm and heel of the hand between the ball and the ground so the ball will rebound into the air on your side of the net. To "dig" effectively you must learn to play the ball low. This gives you more time to place your hand in the proper position for a good pass. The sequence could be described as follows. Determine where the ball is being driven. Move quickly in that direction, taking care not to bend at the waist until you are within reaching distance of the ball. When you have moved to the ball, reach for it, holding the heel of the hand and the flat inner surface of the wrist so that they present as flat a surface as possible to the ball. Remember any knob or irregular surface will cause a deviation in the rebounding characteristic of the ball; therefore cup the wrist rather than extending it.

Spiking the ball is, for most beginners, a very difficult skill to master because it depends upon several critical factors. First a good set is necessary. Only very advanced players learn to hit the "bad" ball while almost anyone can learn to hit a good set. The would-be spiker must learn to move away from the net so that he can hit the ball out in front of his body. Most beginners get caught at the net with the set coming down over their head. When this happens the tendency is to reach over the head and try to hit the ball. Rarely is the ball driven down; usually it is bumped high and slowly goes to the opponent where it is easily fielded. You simply cannot develop a powerful hit of you extend your arm over your head to hit the ball. You must cock the arm and lead out with the elbow just as you do when you throw a ball hard. The volleyball must be contacted well out in front of the shoulder so that the heel of the hand strikes above and behind the center of gravity of the ball. ·

Recently many of the better defensive players have acquired skills at recovering their position after having committed themselves to an extreme effort to field the ball that has resulted in a loss of balance. One of these maneuvers is shown in figure 36. Although there are a number of varia-

Figure 36—Recovery from a Fall

Progress
Can Be Speeded Up

6

A technique for improving individual play that has been used quite effectively involves learning to play with progressively fewer players on a side.

The teams play with the customary six on a side until the rules and most fundamentals of the game are understood. Then the teams are reduced to five on a side for two or three periods of practice, then four, three and finally two. If this progression is timed appropriately, the players become accustomed to moving quickly to the ball and making their passes and sets more effective. After moving through the progression (four to six weeks), the players are reorganized to six on a side. The resultant play is usually dramatically improved since players have learned about the importance of readiness to move and court position. This form of practice also incorporates the improvement of conditioning in a game situation.

Effective serve placement can be developed if the server imagines a six-part division of the court and practices dropping his serve in each one of the six divisions. The skill developed in this kind of practice will enable the server to follow weaker fielders from position to position and force them to move to their weak side to field the ball. Accuracy in serving can also be improved if the server develops a consistent pattern for handling the ball during the preparation for service. This includes details such as the placement of the valve, since the valve causes a slight imbalance which can affect the flight of the ball.

A self-improvement technique which has been helpful in bettering the skills of many news players is called mental practice. This form of practice requires that the individual focus his concentration on patterns of movement he has learned; he introspectively rehearses the skill to be improved. For example, in improving the spike one could introspectively rehearse timing the moving ball with the jump to proper height and the body movements involved in hitting and following through. It has been suggested in various experimental studies that such introspective rehearsal can result in marked improvements in skill. It is a practice widely used by high level performers and can be applied when the individual is away from the game. This focus of concentration can also be helpful in developing the court sense, or the ability to know where and when to move, since you can analyze imagined game situations involving a variety of problems.

The development of specific skills and fundamental maneuvers can best be accomplished by practicing them purposefully in drills which are game-like. Following are examples of how fundamentals can be incorporated into patterns which will be similar to game situations. The symbol key is as follows:

────────▶ passed ball

–⊖–⊖→ player moves

Figure 37—Symbol Key

– – – –▶ set ball

spike or serve

Figure 38— Passing Drill

1. The formation in figure 38 is used to practice passing and setting to various distances and locations. Center player passes to each player in the formation. At the conclusion of a full circuit center then moves to #2 while #1 moves to the center; all other players move one position clockwise.

Figure 39—Multiple Skill Drill

2. The formation in figure 39 can be used to practice pass, set, spike and blocking or digging. The pass from #1 is received by #3 who sets to either #2 or #4 for a spike. The defense can field the ball or attempt a two- or three-man block. All players rotate after two or three turns in the same position. Note: bad passes to the setter and bad sets to the spiker should be played as if a point were at stake.

Can you cause five consecutive serves to land within eighteen inches of the right side line? of the left side line?

3. The formation in figure 40 uses service, service receiving and passing.

It is important to remember that the drills should involve the application of skill in ways very similar or identical to the game situation and that the same effort should be put into practice as into a game.

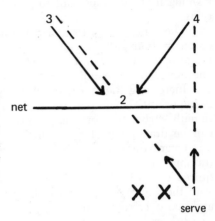

Figure 40—Game Situation Drill

4. A simple drill for developing ability to recover balls from the net is shown in figure 41.

Player A passes the ball into the net at various heights and distances from player B who must then move into position to field it and bump it into the air, preferably as a set since the ball in the net usually occurs on a bad pass and only one hit will remain after the recovery.

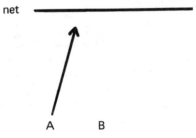

Figure 41—Net Recovery Drill

The development of strength and endurance for improved play can be developed if attention is paid to a few basic concepts. First, the analysis of the players movements must be made in order to establish which major functional muscle groups are being used. These functional muscle groups should then be worked to maximal levels and subsequently *overloaded*. That is, they must be progressively worked harder and harder while going through the identical ranges of motion required during play. This overloading can be accomplished by increasing the intensity of the exercise through the use of additional resistance. Several kinds of apparatus using weights, springs, pulleys, etc. can be used.

The strength in jumping, for example, can be developed by jumping into the air from a ¾ squat position, while carrying weight on the shoulders or around the waist. The jumper could overload by increasing the weight he carries, increasing the number of times he jumps or decreasing the time it would take to jump a given number of times. It is important to jump in the same manner that would be used in the game. During this type of training it is also important to practice the movement under normal conditions.

The arm action in spiking can be duplicated on wall pulley apparatus or on friction pulleys such as the Exergenie. The movement through the range of motion against a resistance will result in increased strength and endurance if the conditioning is carried out in a conscientious manner.

Increasing the resistance progressively over a period of several weeks is important. If the players work to the limits of their strength and continually strive to work just a little harder each time the training effect can be dramatic and play can improve as a result.

Overloading can also be applied by increasing the duration of the training program or by increasing the rate at which the players are required to work. If the players keep track of their progress they will know that they are getting stronger, have more endurance, and are quicker and more effective in their play.

Remember that the player must condition himself for the *specific* muscular and skill requirements of volleyball. Practice does not necessarily make perfect performance. *Only perfect practice leads to perfect performance.*

Language and Lore
of Volleyball

7

Volleyball originated in the United States in 1895 and has gained such popularity through the world that it was included by the Japanese, as host country, in their 17 selections for the 1964 Olympic Games for both men and women. There have been considerable improvements in the two pieces of equipment necessary to play the game since it was first devised by William C. Morgan, a student at Springfield College and later director of the Holyoke, Massachusetts, YMCA. Prior to Morgan's graduation, he devised an idea for a new game which he called minonette. Borrowing skills from tennis, handball and baseball, he erected a tennis net at a height of 6'6" across the center of the gym. A rubber bladder from a basketball was used for the ball. Any number of players were allowed on each team and the object of the game was to hit or bat the ball back and forth over the net. The game was played in nine innings and each server had three outs before his team lost the ball.

Morgan took his game to his first job and introduced it to business-men as a relaxing game, somewhat less strenuous than basketball. It was well received and in 1898 was reviewed, renamed "volleyball" and published in the proceedings of the Springfield College YMCA Sports Conference of that year.

Morgan also wrote the A. G. Spaulding & Bros. Company the specifications for a more suitable ball and there has been no appreciable change made in its design in the 70 years since that time. The official net used at this time is lighter than the tennis net and affords resiliency so that players can pick up a rebounding ball.

The YMCA instructors learned the game at Springfield but as they took it to the various YMCA's around the country they made modifications and revisions in the rules to accommodate special needs.

The original rules recorded in 1896 called for the game to be played in nine innings on a 25' x 50' court. The top of the net was supposed to be 6'6" off the ground and the ball 27" in circumference with a weight of nine to twelve ounces. The server stood with one foot on the back line and had two chances to bat the ball over the net. He was allowed assistance on his serve but no dribbling. A point could be scored only by the server. A net ball, after the first serve, or a line ball, was considered "out." Players could not touch the net or hold the ball and could dribble within only four feet of the net. A ball rebounding from any object outside the court was still in play.

In 1900 the YMCA brought volleyball to Canada, Central and South America and to the Orient, where it was not very popular for many years but is now widely played. In 1900 the YMCA Physical Directors Society adopted a new set of rules which eliminated the dribbling, first bounce and the innings. The game was now played to 21 points over a 7-foot net. The line ball was declared good and the ball could no longer be played off objects outside of the court.

Volleyball was introduced in Cuba in 1905, at the first annual convention of the Playgrounds of America Association (now the National Recreation Association) in 1907 and in Puerto Rico in 1909.

In 1912 the YMCA appointed a special committee to recommend rule changes. This committee moved the net higher, to 7'6", and made it 3 feet wide. The court was enlarged to 35' x 60' and a rule was devised for rotation of players. The serve could no longer touch the net and the two-game match was originated.

One rule which has remained virtually the same and which signifies the spirit of volleyball was recorded during the first YMCA Open Invitational Tournament held at Germantown, Pennsylvania, in 1912—the players called their own fouls. This annual tournament was held for the next ten years.

The education profession recommended volleyball for all school and recreation programs in 1915 because its value as a team sport was realized, together with baseball, basketball and football. During the ten years that followed numerous rule changes were made. In 1917 the net was placed at eight feet and a game played to 15 points. The next year the six-man team was established. In 1921 the center line was put under the net and in 1922 the rule for hitting the ball only three times on each side was introduced. The court was made 30' x 60' in 1923 and it was decided that a team had to make two points in succession to win if the score reached 14-all. This rule was revised in 1925 to read that a team needed two points more than the other team in order to win if the score reached 14-all.

The evolution of the game to its present form was completed by 1925 and included the 8-foot net, six-man team, the marking of a center line, three hits on a side, 30' x 60' court and the 15-point game, with ties at 14-14 being settled by a two-point margin.

Volleyball is generally supported and controlled through the direction of the United States Volleyball Association, which includes representation from other interested groups such as the YMCA, Armed Forces, National Collegiate Athletic Association (NCAA), Amateur Athletic Union (AAU), American Association for Health, Physical Education and Recreation (AAHPER), etc. The volleyball association was organized in 1928 by Dr. George Fisher who is known as the "Father of Volleyball" and who from 1917 until his retirement in 1953 was the editor of the first Volleyball Guide published by the American Sports Publishing Co. of New York. The NCAA and the YMCA worked jointly with Dr. Fisher in editing the rules for the first Volleyball Guide which today serves to describe volleyball activities in all parts of the United States and which has been edited and published annually by the USVBA since the formation of that organization. A system for standardizing tournaments, qualifying officials and selecting representative teams has also been developed by the USVBA.

Volleyball as an international sport owes much of its prominence to the U.S. Armed Forces, which, as early as 1919, had distributed over 16,000 volleyballs to the American Expeditionary Force and its allies (USVBA Guide, 1965). During World War II our servicemen carried the game all over the world. It is now played in more than 60 countries by more than 50 million people. It is the leading sport in 25 countries and ranks third internationally. The sport is especially popular in Japan and Europe. The first world's championship was held in Moscow's Dynamo Stadium in 1952. Julien Lenoir,[2] then Secretary-Treasurer of the International Volleyball Federation which was formed in 1947, noted that 99 per cent of the 60,000 spectators understood the rules and appreciated the performance of the players in those games. The Federation, located in Paris, governs international rules and the annual world's volleyball championship. It is ironic that an American volleyball team has never won a world championship even though volleyball in this country has celebrated its seventieth anniversary. This curious fact is due, in part, to the development of a difference in rules and interpretation in European volleyball that has led to an advanced style of play which has been difficult for Americans to accept.

The enthusiasts in any sports area develop a jargon or specialized language to cover the specific skills and their applications in the games. Volleyball is no different and, although the jargon changes from one part of the country to another, the terms which are covered here are common to most places where volleyball is played extensively.

As the game opens, the six players on each team are arranged in rotation order with three front court and three back court players. Since this rotation order must be observed at the time of service, it is common to see a *switch* occur. This switch allows a temporary rearrangement of players after the serve and permits a spiker and setter in the front court to exchange positions so that the setter is between two spikers. From this position the setter can set the ball to either side. A *back-set* can be used to set the ball up to the spiker behind the setter. This advanced skill is somewhat difficult to execute in a *clean* manner. This term refers to a ball's being distinctly hit, that is, it may not be carried, handled or juggled while it is in play. Examples of plays which are not clean are a *double*, or double hit, wherein the ball is played with one hand or touches another part of the body before it is contacted by the other hand, or a *throw* in which the player has a delayed contact with the ball. This is also referred to as *sticky* ball handling. The development of a pair of clean hands takes a great deal of practice. Concern about consistent rulings on clean plays had led to the virtual elimination of plays in which the open hand or hands are used to field the ball below the waist. Even though many beginners find it more simple to use open hands in an underhand motion to field low balls, it is wise to avoid this habit. While it is easier at first, it becomes a distinct source of trouble as your play improves. It is much better to learn to *bump* or *dig* the ball as described in the skills section of this booklet. The dig, as a skill, was probably developed on the beaches in Southern California where it is common to see *two-man* volleyball played on sand courts. This extremely fast and highly skilled play results in many occasions where the players dive headlong along the sand to field the ball, thus digging it and keeping it in play.

During play it is not uncommon to hear words with special meanings. Frequently when a ball is spiked one of the blockers will call *one*. This means that the ball was hit or touched by one or more of the blockers and that only two hits remain to return the ball over the net. Occasionally a spiker, seeing that he is confronted by a good block, will *dink* the ball. The dink is a light tap that drops the ball just over and behind the block. It is for this reason that one player is usually assigned to *cover* the block, meaning that he must be prepared to move into the area behind the block to field the "dink."

If a spiker runs too far under a set he may change his hitting style to a *roundhouse*. In this maneuver the spiker swings a straight arm in an arc until he contacts the ball, thus imparting a topspin to the ball with a good deal of force. It is effective as change of pace and will sometimes be used as a serving technique as well.

The spiker can also hit either *off hand* or *on hand* depending on whether the ball crosses in front of the body before it is hit. *On hand* means the ball is contacted before it crosses in front of the body.

A player who touches the net will call *net*, thus indicating that play should stop as result of his foul. It is expected that the individual call this foul on himself in the best tradition of the game even though this is not required in the rules. This tradition has been a part of the game since the early 1900's when volleyball tournaments became better regulated and formalized. This custom of calling fouls on one's self has been a key factor in improving the level of play in beach volleyball where it is usually impractical to have an official. Players develop the habit of calling "throws" as well as net violations. The player who does not call his own fouls soon finds it difficult to play with the better players. *Jungle ball,* a loose form of volleyball in which mishandled balls are accepted, is not acceptable to players who are knowledgeable about the game.

Contributions to playing techniques have been developed internationally. The *spike*, for example, is reputed to have been introduced by a little-known team in a tournament in Manila.[3] This "backwoods" team had the habit of passing the ball high in the air so that a large, rangy bushman could run in and hit it. The opposing teams had no defense for this maneuver and, since it did not violate any existing rules, it has developed into a highly-skilled art, the practice of which makes the game an exciting spectator as well as participant sport. Dr. Charles McCloy, a researcher from the University of Iowa, published material stating that a volleyball spike travels an average of 62 m.p.h. with exceptional shots attaining speeds of 110 m.p.h.[4] Recent material, in an attempt to corroborate these findings, has indicated that the maximum speeds are, however, considerably less than 110 m.p.h. Yet the point remains that spikes traveling nearly 100 feet per second require a high degree of defensive skill and quick action if they are to be recovered.

A recent innovation which had its beginnings in Europe has been largely responsible for the success of the Japanese women's Olympic team. They have developed great skill at diving to field the ball and then tumbling back to their feet to be ready for the next play. In tournament play it is remarkable that a spike rarely hits the floor without contact by a defensive player.

Some players, in fact, become so adept at diving for the ball that they can cover a large court area with amazing speed. These players are rarely injured since they have worked on these efforts as a skill and have confidence in their ability to perform the maneuver.

Many innovations have also been developed as a result of the refinements in the game as it is played on the beaches, particularly in Southern California. The court dimensions are regulation but only two players are available to cover this space. In recent years, two-man women's play has improved to the point where the play is nearly as fast and aggressive as the game played by the males. This type of play has, in fact, been instrumental in the revision of women's rules until they have become very similar to the men's. Within the women ranks an identical set of playing rules has been developed for most levels of competition and a strong central organization functions within the United States Volleyball Association.

One of the areas of great weakness in volleyball in the United States, however, centers in the school framework. Even though the game is widely played and widely taught, the technique for higher levels of play have frequently been neglected. This is usually due to a lack of understanding on the part of the teacher who finds the game easy to control and teach to the point where everyone enjoys it. The progress in skill development at this point is dependent upon stressing "clean" ball handling and adherence to the rules concerning play at the net. "Throwing" the ball can be perfected to the point where a player who *might* become a good, "clean" player is reluctant to discard the skills which make him effective in a loosely played game. This lack of attention to progressive development in play unfortunately results in relatively little improvement during the junior and senior high school days.

8 Unwritten Laws

Most sports have certain unwritten rules which add flavor to the game. Volleyball is no exception; for example, there is the custom that a player calls his own fouls. During play it is correct, and usually expected, for a player who fouls to indicate the foul and stop play. The calling out of the word "net" indicates (a) that a player touched the net or (b) that the serve touched the net. This habit, acquired by most players, is universally accepted and the person who fails to call his own fouls is soon out of favor. Even during top competition players will raise their hands if they touch a ball going out of bounds or if they have knowingly committed a fault.

Another instance involves the use of open hands while playing the ball below the waist. The rules state that the ball must be distinctly hit. Obviously this can be done with open hands, but in practice the question of the rigidity of the hands has become a sore point. A player who uses the flat open hand(s) to strike the ball will almost invariably be called for "throwing" or "lifting" the ball. The rejection of this type of play may well come from an attempt to overcome bad habits acquired when individuals were permitted to use an underhand toss to guide the ball during play at the grammar school level, and until recently in the girls' rules where a player was permitted to "set up to self," that is, a toss followed by a second hit. At any rate a good practice to follow is to close hands when playing the ball below the waist. This habit will result in cleaner play and will permit the individual to learn the techniques of "bumping" the ball in the forearm bounce pass. This technique is gaining a great deal of popularity and is used almost exclusively in better competition.

A long tradition of good sportsmanship in volleyball has led to an unusual lack of squabbles as a result of a judgment call by an official. Booing and bad conduct in general are rarely witnessed and a quality of friendly rivalry is present at all levels of play. Heckling and other forms of verbal abuse are nonexistent in the game and a person who uses these tactics is soon reminded that such behavior is inappropriate.

Facts for Enthusiasts 9

The selection and care of volleyball equipment is relatively simple since there is so little to deal with other than the ball and the net.

The net is a specialized variety three feet wide and thirty-two feet long. It has a black, four-inch square mesh body with double thickness canvas across the top. One-quarter inch manila rope usually is used for suspending the nets, although tournament requirements call for a 7,000 pound, one-fourth inch aircraft cable in the top and three-sixteenth cable of 2,000 pound test for the bottom in order to insure uniformity. A two-inch vertical tape on the nets marks the court boundary. In addition a three-foot section of three-fourth inch dowel or broomstick is fastened to each end of the net to permit uniform stretch. The net is not permitted to sag more than a quarter-inch in the middle. This usually requires turn-buckle attachments, although the rope is adequate for most play if it is tightened regularly.

The care of a net is a difficult matter since most preservatives have a base which tends to stain the ball. The best advice is to remove the nets and store them indoors when they are not in use and to follow the adage "a stitch in time saves nine" when a cord begins to fray.

A volleyball is 27 inches in circumference with or without a rubber bladder and with a leather, laceless cover. The official rules call for a twelve panel ball which weighs between 250 and 280 grams. The ball is inflated to insure a rebound vertically between 60-65 inches when dropped from 100" onto a concrete floor. Measurements are from the bottom of the ball. These specifications insure that the balls will have similar playing qualities. Adequate pressure adds to ball life. Lists of "approved" balls are found in the USVBA guide. There are other balls on the market including one which has a greater number of panels (to reduce the tendency for imbalance) and many rubber balls. The rubber balls, while adequate for most play, have never been accepted by the better players since there are subtle differences which disturb them. The rubber balls wear well but have the tendency to become slick with use. In cold weather there is also the tendency for rubber to sting when it strikes the arms or hands.

A good leather volleyball may appear to be expensive ($12-20), but its improved playability is well worth this investment. The life of the ball can be lengthened if care is taken to play on smooth surfaces (cement is generally not a smooth surface), and if it is cleaned occasionally with saddle soap.

The costume for volleyball consists of a pair of lightweight gym shoes with good gripping soles and a uniform which permits a great deal of freedom of movement. The latter is particularly important because the bending and stretching maneuvers are quite extreme and improper dress results in restriction, not to mention the problem of ripping. Some players prefer a long sleeved shirt to protect the arms and cushion the forearm pass.